Muzzled No More

How I came out of Sexual Abuse

Lisa A. Gettings

CONTENTS

INTRODUCTION

May the information in this book shed enlightenment and encouragement to those who have raped, violated, or molested. By sharing my testimony of incest, it will give the readers of this book, that they too can come out and that its ok to come out of place of shame and hurt and be a voice in this hour that we are living in. One of things that kept me silent for so long was shame. I was terrified of speaking out to being molested and violated because I felt no one would believe me and the number one reason was What will people say or think about me? Just know that if you don't speak out that this same violent act will pass on to your child/children to another generation. This should be one of reason why you should be heard. Think about next generation to come, you don't want them to battle the same demons you had to. This too was something I had to think about. I look at my grand-children in their innocence and I tell myself that this must stop right here with me. So those of reading this book find the courage and boldness to stump on devil head. He is a liar and author of lies. You will find that after all this time the cycles you have been in have come from generations curses before you. Where our forefathers in times past open the door to sin and because of ignorance or knowingly cause an open door to curses to come in. These spirits are called familiar spirits. Familiars Spirits are spirits that identify will sins of the family. Therefore, you see same cycles you are in, you see it in your mother, father, aunts, all through your bloodline. For me, when I look back and took notices of my bloodline, I recognized spirits incest, molestation, rape, lesbianism, alcoholism, single-parents, marriage ending as soon as they begin. These are spirits I am talking about. Go back into your family history and recognize your family demons, it will become clearer to you as of why you had to go through what you been through. May you have an Ahh! Moment. Many of you will come of the imprisonment of Satan grip and find hope and stability in the grace and love of Christ. The blood of Jesus is strong enough and powerful enough to break all generational curses. If you cut the root of the tree off, the rest of tree will die. The root is where fruit, branches and leaves get its nourishment from. The tree represents families, kind of like a family tree. By choosing to be a bloodline breaker for your family, you literally can change generations to come.

Chapter 1

Family Secrets

Isaiah 60:1
Arise and Shine for your light has come and the Glory of the Lord Has Risen upon You

I encountered sexual abuse at the young age of 8 up until my late teens at the hands of several family members, and then violated by my stepfather. My first encounter with molestation happened when I stayed the night over a cousin's house, and the next one was by my stepfather. I never knew my father. My stepfather at the time would secretly come into my room at night after everyone was asleep. After so many years, I still hear the quietness of the night as he would silently turn the doorknob so as not to wake anyone. He would quietly make his way under my covers doing things that ought not to be done to little girls. He would touch me, fondle me, and kiss me as if I was his girlfriend or wife. I could never understand for years why he would want to even go after a child, especially when my mother was only a few steps from my room, asleep. Some of you may or may not remember the movie, *Precious*; it came out in 2009. I could relate a lot to Precious story, especially when her mother's boyfriend would violate her and she would take her mind somewhere else so she wouldn't have to feel what was going on with her at that moment. She would dream of being a famous movie star, walking the boardwalk in all its lights and glamour, then reality sets in and she finds that it was just a fantasy. I wouldn't know until later after reading a book by Apostle Ivory Hopkins that this was called "splitting." Splitting is when you cause your mind to drift to another place during sexual relation. There was a time I hated sex and would just do it out of obligation because that's what you do when your mate wants to have sex. I never liked to be touched; it was a reminder of my abuse and violation by my stepfather. I had a hard time trusting people and letting my guard down. Being in my forties, and now looking back over my life as a quiet, shy, timid young lady, I couldn't even wrap my mind around the reality of this one question, Why? Wait! I'm confused; aren't parents supposed to protect their children and not harm them? Aren't they supposed to love them, protect them from the very person who would do these bad things to me? I could only think of wanting him to finish his business and I would curl up in fetal-like position, wondering why? Why me? Why is this happening to me? Now, as an adult, I can now share my testimony in the hope of helping someone else find freedom. I remember so vividly taking long showers, because in my mind, I just didn't feel clean enough. I scrubbed myself over and repeatedly, as the shower of water hid my tears of anguish and pain. I just couldn't get clean enough. Why couldn't I get clean? Thoughts of fear, suicide, and shame would run to and fro in my mind. I went to grab a knife to slice my wrist in hopes that the pain I was suffering would go away. After all, who would notice me anyway? No one loved me, no one cared for me; I felt worthless as these thoughts run through my mind, but I just didn't have the guts to kill myself. Why did God let me live through this? The even bigger question is, *Why am I here anyway?* Something so horrific and unimaginable. He would continue to do this horrible act for many years following. I felt like a dirty rug that someone can just wipe their feet on anytime they wanted to. Once or twice a week, he would continue to abuse me. He would keep me quiet by buying me things, taking me to stores, giving me money, my first car, and an array of other gifts to shut me up. I didn't know then as a young lady that this was hush money. This is what sexual predators do to keep their victims quiet—they buy you things or threaten you so they can continue with their victimization of you. I would have this inward desire to say something but thoughts of 'who-would-believe-you' would enter my mind. Fear would grip me so bad that I felt as though if I said anything, what would people say or think of me? Or even if they believe, I had no one to turn to; no one I could share this secret with. Everybody looked up to this man, but if they only know his desires to violate girls, they would probably change their minds. I carried the secret for so many years. I feigned fine, walking around with a smile on my face, but inwardly, I had secret battles, scars, and pain. Each day was a miracle for me to even wake up. I just wanted to die and didn't have the courage to kill myself. Whenever I hear of other people's stories of sexual abuse, they either turned to drugs, alcohol, or sexual promiscuity. I found relief and comfort in eating too much, watching too much T.V., and thumb sucking. Yes, sucking my thumb was something I would use to find comfort, to sleep or if I found myself in a situation where I became nervous, I would revolt to thumb-sucking. I would hide what I was really going through, by laughing and smiling—that was my way of getting through life. This is the mask I would put on to hide my brokenness and shame.

Chapter 2

Rejection

Psalm 27:10

When your mother and father forsake you, then the Lord will take you up.

I experienced a lot of rejection from people at a young age. Rejection entered my life at an early age when the sexual abuse first started. I would find out from reading books on rejection that the fear of rejection, self-rejection, and rejection, is a three-fold cord that is not easily broken. Fear of rejection is when a person convinces themselves that they need no one and can do what needed to be done all by themselves. Truly, a person like this has been rejected somewhere in their life. It is just a defense mechanism to keep from being hurt again. Everyone wants to be accepted and loved. So, I go through life with the fear of rejection, not even trying to get close to anyone because they may reject me. They may try to get close and reach out to me; I just wouldn't receive it, and now, that person is rejected by my action. Self-rejection is when a person rejects him/herself. I used to think no one loved me. I had low self-esteem and felt that no one would want to love a person like me. I didn't know my identity in Christ. I would reject myself and others before I even try to let others in. All three of these: rejection, self-rejection, and fear of rejection are all breeding grounds for demonic strongholds. Pigs in a Parlor by Fred and Ida Mae Hammond gave an awesome example of how rejection operates in a person's life. Take a tree for example; the root of the tree is rejection. It starts inward, while branches, stems, and leaves are the outward behavior that stems from rejection like rebellion, perversion, lust, alcohol, drugs, and many other behaviors that causes a person's life to go on a downward spiral. It all stems from rejection happening in that individual's life from a young age, even from the womb if you were adopted or you were an unwanted child. Some of us deal with rejection by being introverts and never letting anyone in; others have an outburst of anger to compensate for rejection while some like myself were both. I would go into my shell and then when I felt rejected by people, I would get furious and try to comfort myself by overeating to calm my nerves down. In fact, if I can be transparent here, I remember several times going off on my daughter in a fit of rage. I will never forget the fear and terror in her eyes. I can say I really didn't know why but a part of me knows that she was a reminder of the abuse I suffered at the hands of her father. She looked so much like him. She didn't deserve to be hit like that. She had a mother that was suffering on the inside, and I know that she receives a lot of rejection by me. I didn't know how to give her the love she deserved after being rejected by my own mother. I never experienced love in my household; we want huggers or should I say the 'I-love-you' type of family, but she loved through it all. Later in my walk with God, as He began to bring inner healing, I would ask her forgiveness for things I said and did to her. I am getting better in my love walk with people. It has been challenging, but I refuse to isolate and reject myself or others anymore. Either people receive me or not, I am accepted in the beloved. When my mother and father forsake me, then the Lord will take me up (Psalm 27:10; KJV).

In school, I got good grades, and you would never think there was an issue at home and I only had two friends. I felt that I was different from most kids. I never really fitted in or was liked by most—only a few classmates. No matter how much I tried, I could never fit in and I wondered why people didn't like me? When I didn't fit in, I felt rejected by people and would go into deep, sad depressions at times, and cry myself to sleep. We all want love and acceptance by others. I would convince myself that I didn't need anyone, that I can do it all by myself. That was my way of putting a wall up around myself and my heart to keep me from getting hurt or rejected by anyone. I would later find out what kind of life this really would be, never receiving love from genuine people who wanted to get to know and love the real Lisa. I guess I looked at love as something people would say until they get what they wanted from me and then leave. I never experienced real love until God came down and found me in the midst of all my pain. I wouldn't see this for many years though; even then, I would trust God only with the portion of my heart that I wanted to give Him, whereas He wanted all of me. I never could receive the love people had for me because of my outlook or thinking on what love is— which was corrupted by abuse.

As a matter of fact, when anyone would hug me, my skin would literally cringe because it took me back to the inappropriate touch of my abuser. The thought of anyone loving me was unbearable, because I didn't love myself. Besides, if I open myself up and they reject me, which was something I just wasn't willing to gamble on. This man that took the place of my real father was only a father figure I had in my life. Every girl child wants to be daddy's little girl. Later, as I got older, I would ask my mom about who my real father was. From the story she told, it seems as if he too had his own private battles. Growing up, I was a very shy, quiet, timid, and sensitive individual. I hated to be yelled at because it made me feel like I couldn't do anything right. Even though that might not have been that person's intention, but in my mind, that's how I felt. I never really had enough confidence in myself to speak up for me. This would come much later in my journey with the Lord. I was afraid to even tell my mother that the man she picked up off streets somewhere or from a night of clubbing or after a drunken binge, was abusing me.

Single moms, this is a warning for you! Be careful of men you bring into your home after a night of drinking and clubbing and all of a sudden, you wake up the next day and have this strange man in your bed that you don't even remember bringing him home with you and now, you and him are boyfriend/girlfriend. You are not aware you just let a sexual predator into your house and while you're at work, you left him alone with your child to babysit, and you got to know the truth years later when your child have the courage to tell you, but you are surprised and thrown back regarding why he or she didn't divulge sooner. How many of you remember playing moms and dads? While your parent had company over, and they are drinking and playing cards, and you and other kids are playing mom and daddy. One person is the mother, another is the daddy and you do what mother and daddy do, that's right, you kiss and fondle. This can also open sexual abuse. Parents, if you recognize your child behavior has changed, and they are acting out in school and home, withdrawing to themselves when they used to be outgoing, pay attention. These are some signs that your child may be sexually abused. These signs may not be the case in all situation; it could be something else bothering the child. I am just saying pay close attention to your children and who you let into your home. Also, know who your kids spend the night with.

I have a section in this book on warning signs to look for if your child is being abused. Every sexual abuse situation is different but these are just a few basic signs. In my situation, I was good at suppressing it; I didn't want to remember. I was being tormented in my mind and looking for love in wrong relationships. I kept my conversations with people short so they don't ask questions because I didn't want them to know what I was dealing with. I had this cousin on my stepfather's side that would always call me her cousin even though my mother and step-father weren't married. I love staying at her house on weekends. It was one place where I could find peace from my stepfather even if it was just a couple of days. When it was time to leave, I dreaded.

Years later, I found that my cousin too was raped by a man her mom brought into the house. You see, my mother and I never had a mother-daughter relationship at all. She was very strict and I never could do anything. As a single mom, I believed she did the best she could with what she had to work with. I had better than most kids had it. I had a roof over my head, clothes on my back, and food on the table. I don't blame her and have forgiven her. Her one shortfall was that she would drink and lease her anger out on me. She was like a raged lion gnawing into its prey until it was consumed. This was the type of environment I lived in. I didn't even trust her enough to go and tell her anything.

One thing the enemy does is isolate and make you think that nobody cares about you. The very people you thought you could trust enough to go talk to, like a parent, even reject you. What do you do when you get rejected in your own house? The sexual abuse was enough but physical abuse on top of that was sufficient to make anyone go insane. I never remember my mother hugging and telling me she loved me while growing up. That would come years later. Better late than never, I guess. Later, I would find that I am my mother's daughter. Generational curses are something that we will deal with later in another chapter.

Chapter 3

God's True Purpose For Me

Part of me as I got older wondered how my mother could not realize that this man she brought into our home was a sexual predator. Why didn't she notice the way he looked at me? The way he would buy me things, or the way he defended me against her? The devil is sneaky, cunning, and manipulative. My answer to these questions are found in 1 Peter 5:8 that says, *be sober, be vigilant because your adversary the devil walketh about as a roaring lion seeking whom he may devour*. The devil uses people as puppets to bring havoc and destruction on the family because he is against anything that is good, lovely, and of good report. The demon of sexual perversion that had come into my stepfather's life through an open door was using him to destroy my destiny in Christ. The devil thought he had a well-planned, thought-out, shatter-proof assignment for my life. For every demise he had planned for my pitfall would bring coals of fire on his own head. You see the part of you that Satan wants to kill, is God's purpose for your life that He placed on the inside of me and you. If he can keep and make you feel and think that you're worthless, never amounting to anything and that you will never fulfil your dreams because you're dumb, stupid, ugly, fat, thin, worthless, unloved, unwanted, used up, etc., he is close to victory. He can sometimes playback in your mind the tape recorder of negative words your mother, father, siblings, family members, and what people have said about you growing up. This is called memory recall. These words are used by the enemy against you and have it play repeatedly in your minds as a little kid, and some even until our adulthood. Words making us feel invaluable and inferior. It's all lies from the pit of hell. The enemy doesn't want you to find your identity in Christ Jesus. I am writing this book to all that will listen, to every woman who has battled sexual, emotional, and mental abuse. Perhaps you are being abused by husband, father, stepfather, pastor, priest, friend, stranger, sold into child trafficking, violated in any form where another human forced himself on you. I write my story for you today in my first book so you can see who you really are in Christ, and how the enemy came to steal your voice and your identity.

I write this book to encourage you so that you can come out and be set free by the power of God. God has showed me how crucial it was for me to write this book because the people reading this might be bound by the enemy in this area. It might have been 10, 20, 30 years or more and you still have not forgiven your abuser. You still have not forgiven yourself even though it wasn't your fault the accuser forced himself on you but you're still blaming yourself. I have come to bring healing and deliverance through my story so that many of you can come out of that dark pit, that dark pit of desolation, fear, doubt, and shame, and bring hope to you today. I come to set you free from all your fear and doubt that the enemy has used to keep you bound up and have you thinking you will never come out. John 8:36 says he whom the Son set free is free indeed. When you have the Son, you can walk in your freedom and victory that Christ gave you through His death and resurrection. Grab hold of His unchanging love for you. People, sometimes, put conditions on our love for one another; they love you today and hate you tomorrow. However, just know that God's love has no conditions attached to it. He loves us regardless of how we perform. While we were still in our sin, Christ died for us. So, there is nothing you can do to get God to stop loving you. Absolutely nothing! Hallelujah! I love the scripture words in Romans 8. It's one of my favorite scriptures (Romans 8:35-39): *Who shall separate us from the love of Christ? Shall tribulation, or distress, or persecution or famine, or nakedness, or peril, or sword? As it is written, for your sake we are killed all day long, we are accounted as sheep for the slaughter. No, no in all these things we are more than conquerors through him that loved us. for I am persuaded, that neither death, nor life, or angels, or principalities, nor powers, nor things present, nor things to come, nor height, nor depth, nor any other creature, shall be able to separate us from the love of God, which is in Christ Jesus our Lord.* Hallelujah!

God doesn't love you more than He already does right now. Receive His love today; receive His forgiveness today, my sister, in the name of Jesus. For so long, the devil has tried to kill you; he has tried to take your voice, and hinder you from getting into divine destiny, but I decree and declare over your life, that your light has come, your deliverance has come, and you will live and not die and declare the works of the Lord. I take the muzzle off your mouth; you will no longer be muzzled or silenced by the enemy any longer in the name of Jesus. For the Lord has not given you a spirit of fear but of love, power, and a sound mind. I say rise, stand up and be a voice in the place God had called you to walk in, in Jesus' Name. You will live to share your story in the land of the living and will not take your story to the grave until all has been fulfilled in your life and you will be silent no more, in Jesus' Name.

Listen to me! Your past doesn't have to dictate your future. It was set up for your comeback!! It's never too late; you can begin again. I say you can begin again. You are never too old to do what God called you to do. What would have taken you years to fulfill, God can do it in an instant. He is not limited by time. There is no beginning nor end; God is not limited by our age, past failures, or bad decisions to bring His promise to fulfilment in your life. Psalms 37:25 says have been young and now I am old, yet I have never seen the righteous forsaken, nor his seed begging bread. Those that hope in the Lord, He will renew their strength according to Isaiah 40:31. If you have breath in your body, no matter how many years have passed, God has invested everything in you. He is in it for the long term because He believes in the investment He deposited in you. You can come out and have a good, successful, and purposeful life. I am a witness to that life. I never thought God could use a shy, timid, broken African-American from the backside of the mountains of Virginia in a small town called Buena Vista Virginia, but God chose me. I am an entrepreneur, and in a few months, I will be ordained as a pastor and now, I'll be a published author. I give God all the honor and praise that is due to His holy name. Hallelujah!!!

Yes, bad things have happened to you; life has dealt you a deck of cards that you never asked for, but dream again my sister, dream again my daughter. This time you want to fail, but how long are you going to stay in that victim mentality? Tell yourself; I will no longer be a victim but a Victor. This person that abused you have moved on with his life, and you're still holding on to your past to something that happened 5, 10, 15, 20 years ago or longer. In Philippians 3:13, Paul says, *I count not myself to have apprehended it but this one thing I do, forgetting those things which are behind and reaching forth unto those things which are before me.* It is time to look forward and not behind; leave the past right where it's in the past and never remember or pick it up again. What's in front of you is bigger than what you can ever imagine or think. God is about to restore everything you lost in your past. You see, God wants to see us set free in every area of our lives. Spirit, soul, body, finances, family, children, marriage, etc. Some of you have been abused sexually and never told your husband. He thinks he is the reason he can't please you sexually, but it's really because you never told him of the abuse. I pray that God will give you the courage to tell him the truth. The enemy wants to magnify your situation like a magnifying glass when you look through it; it makes what you are looking at bigger so that he can keep you in fear, but there is nothing too big or hard for God that He cannot fix. If your husband loves you and took his vows to you serious, he will understand and help you through the process. My prayer is that every person reading this book would rise in their inner man, inner being, and make the decision of coming out of the prison of sexual abuse. When you do, this God will heal your broken heart; He will set you free from your tormentors and you will experience a freedom in your life that you have never experienced before.

Mathew 11:28 (King James Version): *"Come all who are weary and heavy laden and I will give you rest. Take my yoke upon you and learn from me, for I am gentle and humble in heart and you will find rest for your soul. For my yoke is easy and my burden is light."* Come and give it all to Jesus; He will give you that rest that you cannot find in a man, alcohol, drugs, money, etc. It is time to stop hiding; it is time to stop being a victim. For healing to take place, you must admit what happened to you. When I decided not to be quiet anymore, that was when I saw my healing come. I didn't want to admit it at first; I would suppress it and behave like it didn't happen. The more I talked about it, I found more and more freedom but not just that, God sent a woman to me who had been through sexual abuse. I realize my story isn't just for me and my family but for others as well. Christ came and heal the brokenhearted and set the captives free (Luke 4:18).

Don't you want to be whole? Don't you want to be free? Aren't you tired of crying yourself to sleep at night? Come to Jesus and find rest for your soul. John 10:10 says it even better; *the thief comes to steal and kill and destroy, I have come that they might have life and that they might have it more abundantly*. God's purpose is to give us a rich and satisfying life. That word "might" means expressing condition or possibility. The word "abundantly" in Greek means excessive, superabundantly, exceedingly abundantly, advantage, beyond measure. Christ has done everything for us that He is going to do. He died on the cross for our sins and rose again on the 3rd day with the keys from death and hell. He rose with all power in His hand. It's up to us to grab hold of the precious promises of the word of God and apply it to our lives. No one is going to do it for you. That word might be contingent on you. You make that decision to recognize who your real enemy is; you make the decision that you will no longer continue to allow the enemy to sabotage your life.

The Bible says in Ephesians 6:12 that, *for we wrestle not against flesh and blood, but it's against principalities, powers, rulers of the darkness of this world and spiritual wickedness in high places.* It took me years to finally find out why my life was so defeated. I was fighting the wrong battle. It's a spiritual warfare; we are not in a physical fight. My fight wasn't against people, it wasn't against my stepfather—he was an instrument the enemy used to try to destroy my life until light came on. Satan is a defeated foe and there is no truth in him. So, I had to realize I had an enemy that wanted to kill me. He wanted to take my life; he didn't want me to advance. He didn't want me to experience success and have the good life for which Jesus died. He is against anything that is good. Battles are won fighting my enemies in prayer with the promises of God. Then and only then did scales begin to roll off my eyes, but not only that. I had to recognize who I was in Christ and that I was not all those negative feeling and filthy thinking that the devil put in my head.

The Devil, your real adversary, wants to keep you tied up and tormented by your past so that you don't grab hold of your identity in Christ. He wants your testimony to stay bound in you, covered up in shame, so that other women cannot find freedom in your story. Get your voice back; get your confidence back. Isaiah 61:7 (NIV) says, *"Instead of your shame you will receive double portion. God will take away your shame and he will in turn give double honor."* This is such a powerful scripture. You are not alone, sister. I pray that as you read this book, and read my story, you will find freedom and courage to come out of solitude and jail—the prison that has held you captive by your abuser, and that you will find hope and life again, which can only be found in Christ. After realizing this, I started to see victory, breakthrough, peace, joy, and freedom in all areas of my life. Know that I am not saying that my stepfather got a free pass. What I am saying is that I had to release all anger, bitterness, memories, and torment over to God.

Romans 12:19 says (AMP): *Beloved, never avenge yourself, but leave the way open for God's wrath, for it is written, "Vengeance is Mine, I will repay," says the Lord.* There is no greater avenger than the Almighty God. If we try to avenge ourselves, it is like you taking poison and wanting the other person to die. No sister, you're going die. Give it to Jesus. Jesus took all our sins, shame, and guilt on His own body so that we can live. He did that for me and you. That's how much the Almighty God loves us. My deliverance was not as easy as it sounds. Healing and deliverance is a process. It wasn't an overnight thing. The more I pressed into God, confess scriptures over myself, my life, and going to deliverance conferences, the more God's hand of healing started peeling me back like an onion. An Onion has many thin layers; when God healed me of one thing, He started showing me something else. It takes time to walk in total deliverance. Some get healed instantly and for some, it's a process and for some, it took years because God is never truly done revealing Himself to us. Don't rush the process but trust the process. He is always showing us how much He loves us. He takes the good, the bad, and the ugly, and uses them for His good. Everything good and bad that has ever happened in my life, God used it all for His glory that He may win others to Him through me every time I share my testimony.

Romans 8:28: *And we know that all things God work together for good to them that love God, to them who are the called according to his purpose.* Someone may ask, "So, are you saying God caused this to happen to me?" No! That's not what I'm saying. God is a good God. He gives each of us freedom of choice and will to do what we want because when we come to Him, it will be because we love Him and we are willing to surrender our life to Him. It is not because He forced His will or ways on us. God doesn't go around violating and forcing Himself on His people to do what He wants us to do. That is not love. The person that did this horrible thing to me and you, he/she forced his/her will on me and you. That's not love and it's not of God. Forgive him; forgive yourself. You did nothing wrong. Some of you may be saying, "Perhaps, if I didn't wear my hair a certain way," or "my clothes too tight," or "too much makeup," "perhaps it was the way I talked or carried myself." No!! No!! No!! As I'm writing this book, I literally hear the voice of the Holy Spirit assisting me to write the answer to a lot of your questions.

The next question you have is, "If God love me so much, why didn't He stop it or do something about it?" Some of you reading this book are angry at God, and you don't want anything to do with Him. In fact, you blame

Him for what happened to you. I'm here to tell you that it is okay. I felt the same way too until I got a better understanding of the nature and character of God and how we live in a fallen world. Let me start out by saying as I walk you through this journey of the fall of man, your mind will become clear of just how much God loves you.

In the Book of Genesis, the earth was dark and without form, so God created everything that we see today. In Genesis Chapter 1:26-28, you see the creation called Man and how God gave him dominion over everything He created. They could eat and enjoy everything that God made except the tree of the knowledge of good and evil.

In Chapter 3, we see the fall of man. Satan comes along and convince Eve and gets her to second-guess herself if God truly told her not to eat from the tree of the knowledge of good and evil. She eats the fruit after Satan convinces her and then starts the downfall of man. Satan becomes the god of this world and now has the title meant for Adam who God originally gave the dominion of the earth. This is how man's heart turned so evil. It wasn't like that in the beginning. Man and nature lived in harmony with God. This very sin separated us from having a relationship with God, but all is not lost. God had a plan to get His creation—humanity, back in reconciliation with Him by sending His Son, Jesus, to the earth through a virgin named Mary. God took on human form in the person of Jesus Christ. The Bible says it was God in Christ reconciling the world to Himself (2 Corinthians 5:19). Mathew 12:40 says Jesus spent three days and three nights in the depth of the earth and because He is alive according to Revelation 1:18, where Jesus says, *"I am he that live and was dead and behold, I am alive for evermore, amen, and have the keys of hell and death."* Because He lives, we live. All authority was given to Jesus and when we become born again, His Nature, Life, Holiness, and Wisdom, comes and live in us as we surrender our lives, our ways of living and thinking, and lay it at the foot of the cross. This is what Jesus did for me, you, and all of humanity. Because of shedding of His blood, we have been redeemed from the curse of the law, spiritual death, poverty, sickness, and disease. It's not something we work for, labor for, or earn. It is a gift from God called grace. That gift of Grace where all your sins, past failures, mistakes, shame, guilt was laid on this gift from God, is Jesus. Whosoever call on that name shall be saved. Ephesians 2:8, 9 says for it by grace that we are saved, not of works lest any man should boast. Grace is a gift that we don't deserve or earned. God freely gives it to us. Lest any man should boast or think he can get to God based on his own work, abilities, or merits.

Chapter 4

He is Not the Father

You may know the popular show called *Maury Show*. He would have free DNA testing on the presumably father of the baby and on public T.V. We would find out if the child was his or not. The person who wants the DNA would try to convince the audience that the child looked like the person she wanted it to be by pointing out some features of the father on the child's picture because she wanted it to be his so badly. The results are in and this is the part of the show where everyone is on the edge of their seats, waiting for the results. The envelope is opened and the results says, "You are not the father." The accuser runs off stage because the results are not what she expected and the audience goes wild. What a humiliating time for her! To continue with my story even into my teens, did my stepfather continue to violate me? I started dating a young man, and I really was liking him.

During that time, we moved in together, moving me out of the environment I was in. For so many years, I wanted to escape but really didn't know how but this was my moment of escape, but not until my stepdad had one more encounter with me. After a few months, I realize I wasn't having period and I could no longer buckle up my pants. That's right, I was pregnant. I didn't really know if it was my boyfriend at time or my step farther. I would tell my boyfriend that it was his because I really didn't know for sure until the baby was born. If I told him the truth of the possibility of it being my stepfather, he would reject me and leave. Besides, we were having problems at the time. So, I choose to carry the lie even after the baby was born. Now, the baby girl is here and she looks just like my stepfather, then I knew for sure who it was but I was still ashamed to tell my boyfriend for fear of him leaving.

Days, months, and years roll by. People would say it looked like the guy I was with but I knew that wasn't true. How much longer could I carry this lie with me? It was only a matter of time before it's found out. People would begin to ask questions and look at me funny and stare at the baby, talking under their breath. I was walking on eggshells every day of my life. I was tormented day and night for years. You become tormented when you know you're trying to hold a family secret together to keep it from being exposed. The more I tried to hold it together, the more I was losing my grip. It wasn't worth my life or that of my child. It came to a point where I decided to let go. I wanted God more than anything in my life. Any relationship based on a lie or started with lie will never work out anyway. I wanted God's best, so I had to do it His way. When the relationship ended, God stepped in. When I felt myself fallen, God caught me! I'm so thankful for the love and forgiveness He showed towards me. He raised me up and gave me a testimony. No longer bond; no more chains holding me. I can declare I am free. I have overcome by the blood of the Lamb and the word of my testimony (Revelation 12:11).

Chapter 5

Generational Curses

In the next pages is the story of my daughter and what it was like to be raised by a mother that was abused, hurt, and broken. I wanted to add her to this book as to relate to how generational curses, which sprinkle down from one generation to the next, which occur not because of anything we have done but because of the choice of our forefathers made, can follow a bloodline. I pray that someone who has held a secret such as I did, would come out from hiding, be healed and set free to tell their story too.

Growing up as a child, I always felt that my mother didn't love me. As I grow older, that love became even more distant. I so desperately wanted my mother to say the three words, "I love you," and to hug me ever so tightly and never let go. I was raised in a Christian household. My mother loved the Lord. I've seen her serve faithfully for so many years. But on the other hand, there was another side of her that would come out that just wasn't her. She would serve on Sunday but after that, her personality would change. She would latch out on me for things I didn't do. She would go off on me for no apparent reason. It was like a fit of rage going off inside of her and I was the butt of that rage. It was always me getting in trouble while my brother would get away with everything. I could never figure out why she was one way on Sunday and when we were home, she was a different person.

I remember one time we had to clean a beauty salon. My mother was frustrated about something and took her frustration out on me. I remember her eyes were filled with rage; it was like I didn't even know her. Whenever I wanted to know who my father was, my mother would never tell me until I got into my teens. It was then she told me what happened to her and how she was molested and violated for so many years and I was conceived out of it. She was only protecting me from him. That's why she never let me see him all those years. It answers so many questions for me. I understood why she couldn't love me the way I needed to be loved because she never got the love she needed as a child.

Growing up, I didn't like myself. I was bullied at school, talked about, hit on and called names. I believed everything they said about me. I didn't have much self-esteem. Being rejected at school is one thing but being rejected at home too caused me not to believe in myself. Being born out of incest; I was thankful that my mother didn't abort me. In today's society, it is easy to get an abortion when the situation is fit, but she chose to keep me even though she probably had thoughts of aborting me. Because my mother and I weren't close, I felt I could talk to her. In my teen years, I started to open doors to wrong relationships, masturbation, pornography, sexting pictures to men, chat sites—all to get the attention and exception I wasn't getting at home. Until one day, my mother found my phone and we talked about it, and I remember her grounding me. But I kept mum during those times, only being more careful. When we moved to Oklahoma, I got involved in a dance team at my church. Mrs. Natashia was the dance instructor. I love being on that team. I gained so many friends. I finally found something that made me feel loved and accepted. I felt I belong, and I grow to love God on top of that. Just being on a dance team took everything away that I was going through.

In 2004, I gave my life to Christ and got baptized. As an adult, I still felt the need to have a man in my life. Instead of waiting on God's timing to send me His man, I looked for love in all the wrong places instead of in God. I backslide in my relationship with God.

In 2014, I got involved with a man and conceived my first child. I was hesitant at first, but I went through with it, thinking he would love me but only found disappointment of being in a bloodline where children are conceived out of wedlock with single-parent households. No one is marrying or if they did marry, it never lasted very long. One day, I was feeling lonely and open myself up to chatline where I met a man. He seemed like the perfect gentleman in the beginning. We had sex the first time we met, and I let him move in with me. My life took a downward hell spiral after that. I had my first child by him, then the 2nd in less than a year later.

He started becoming obsessive, controlling, and manipulative. All the signs of a narcissistic personality, only that I didn't know it then. We would fight and argue often. I didn't have any peace in my house. We would break up and then he would smooth-talk me into letting him back in. This went on for several years. All of these was going on in front of my children at the time. My mother would talk to me, but I didn't listen. I wanted what I wanted and really didn't care. I love him and didn't want to be alone. My mother didn't like the situation I had put myself and children in, especially all the fighting and arguing in front of them. She would talk to me, trying to bring me to my senses. I would listen to her, knowing that I wasn't quite ready to let go yet. Because this guy was bigger and stronger than me, when he got angry, I would see his face change. It looked like I was fighting the devil himself and a chill would come over me that put such fear in me, and it would torment me in my sleep. It was like a paralyzing fear. I felt like I wasn't myself. This person that I let into my life and that of my children was controlling my life and decisions. He would have people watch me to see if another man would come over while he was at work.

One day, I lost my keys to my van and apartment. I went out to look for it in my van and someone he had watching me called and told him what I was doing. He came home like a bat out of hell. There was a time he would force sex on me when I didn't want to. So, I would give in to his advances. He would accuse me of cheating even though I wasn't. He would blame everything on me for the relationship going wrong, never looking at himself. He would tell his family and friends all the things I was doing, but never the things he was doing behind closed doors, trying to make himself look good in front of people. It was always everybody else and never him. He was pumped up with pride. My mother once told me that pride is just a cover-up for how he really feels about himself, which is insecurity. He really was insecure and hid behind the spirit of pride. Another tactic he would do is take the keys to my van or damage my van so that I wouldn't go anywhere. He was controlling every aspect of my life. It was an abusive relationship that I didn't know how to get out.

One day, I told my mother I was done and ready to get him out of my life. The light bulb had finally come on. I came to my senses. She didn't believe me at first because I had said it so many times before. She was there for me and my children in the midst of all my troubles. She never gave up on me. I wouldn't be here today if it weren't for having a praying mother. It seemed liked no matter what I tried to do, he wouldn't let go. I broke off our union; he would make a copy of my keys so that he could come into my house anytime he wanted too. My mother studied something on deliverance, so she told me everything I was battling with and that I can overcome them. She helped me through the process of getting rid of him. If anything, I had to do it for my children. It took some time even with all his threats and manipulation. My mother encouraged me to stand up to him. Speak up and tell that devil to get out your life, your home, and out of your children's life because he isn't welcome anymore.

I finally stood up to the devil and let him know I wasn't taking it anymore, and I wasn't scared of him. Gradually, I made my way out of the relationship. He would say he loved me and wanted to be with me. But I wasn't falling for it anymore. I am done!!! I gave my life back to Christ. I kicked him and his demons out of my house. I found the courage to stand up to him. That moment He found out I was scared no more and standing up to him, I noticed he backed down and didn't come around as much. He had moved on to another relationship. I still must deal with his threats to take the kids from me by taking me to court to keep the kids and me from moving on with our life. I just keep telling myself that no weapon formed against me will prosper. I decided not to allow a man into my life until I have completed my healing and deliverance process. I know it will be a long journey, but with God and His presence in my life, I can do all things through Christ who strengthens me. I hope that whoever is reading this will find the courage to stand up to their fears. Stand up to your abuser; stand up and be silent no more. The devil became a wimp when I stood up to him.

If you are in a domestic dispute situation like I was, and your boyfriend is threatening to kill you and your children, I would say, get out now! Maya Angelou says it best, "When someone shows you who they are, believe them the first time." Do whatever you can to get out. Move away. Change your name. Get some help. There is help out there. You are not alone. There are organizations that help in situations such as domestic violence. I am currently in the process of moving from one state to another to get away from him and start over. Thank you for allowing me to share my testimony. I hope that something on the inside of you has shifted to make a change for good and your children.

Chapter 6

Finding Inner Healing

All through my relationship with this man, I would have sudden outburst of anger that would come out of nowhere. I never realized it until I started having sexual relations with this man. I would fly off the handle when I get rejected by him or when things didn't go my way. I was a tea kettle when it reached its boiling point; it starts off with a whistle and steam would pour out of it. Anything could set me off. I remember so vividly going off on my daughter one day with such a fierce anger. The look her in eyes was the same look I would get when my mother would go off on me. I would tell myself I would never treat my children the way I was treated growing up. Yet, here I was, my mother's daughter. Numbers 14:18 says, *"The Lord is slow to anger, abounding in love and forgiving sin and rebellion. Yet he does not leave the guilty unpunished; he punishes the children for the sin of the parents to 3rd and 4th generations."* I love where it says curses go back three or four generations but blessings go forward for a thousand generation. We cannot change things that have occur in our bloodline from our past. Thank God that in Christ, according to Galatians 3:13, Christ has redeemed us from the curse of the law. Any curses that came down from the sins of my father, mother or ancestor, any form of witchcraft and rebellion that opened over my family is broken because Christ redeemed me from it. Anything passed down to me because of my ancestors, mother, or father, due to ignorance or generational curses, it stops right here and now with me in the Name of Jesus. Some things we see going on in our lives is simple because of bad choices, and we are seeing the results of those bad decisions passing on to our children. Rebellion doesn't just affect you, it will affect your children as well. The curse can pass down to children as we see it in the scripture, but someone in the family must get saved and take the word and blood of Jesus to break those curses so it doesn't pass down to our children and our children's children, including the generations to come. God wants to save a whole generation just by using the obedience of one person. So, I look at it like I'm saving a whole generation of Caleb and Joshua who had a different spirit in them. Many reading this book, you are called to be a Moses. Moses delivered the children of Israel out of Egyptian bondage, and you are called to deliver your family. You might not know it yet, but you are. You will deliver not only your family but you are bringing others out with you. That spirit of sexual perversion would continue to operate in a family bloodline as a curse until someone grabs hold of the word of God and starts confessing blessings and making right choices. I decided it would be me, so my children don't have to fight with demons I had to battle with.

Then the day came where I had a personal encounter with Christ. I wasn't raised in a Godly home; my mom was raised in church but backslide for many years. I never remember her ever going to church. I would go to church as a young child when I would go to my grandmother for summer and few other times. I believe in God. Children's church will tell me of God who loves me, but I don't really know what it meant to have a relationship with Christ. All I know is that the day came when I just wanted to be free. I was tired of lies; I was sick and tired of my life and the way it was going. I had a neighbor that moved in a few doors from me; her name is Maria, and she was so bold in sharing Christ with people and how God delivered her from drugs. I must admit I was drawn by the light of Christ in her. How many of you know this was a setup, and a divine appointment from heaven? God know that I was ready and He sent Maria to be that voice for Him that day. She shared Christ with me that day in her home while cooking fish. I remember it like it was yesterday. She prayed the sinner's prayer with me and I said it from my heart this time. I meant it and wanted a change. How many of you in your life had a believer share Christ with you, that you even repeated the sinner's prayer but you know you weren't ready for change or letting go of your sinful life? You said it just so they could leave you alone. After she said the sinner's prayer with me, she invited me to her church. My life has never been the same. It would be a long drawn-out process for me. Just because we give our life to Christ doesn't mean things will change immediately. When we became born again, our spirit was born anew. What does this mean? When we receive Christ in our hearts, the Spirit of God comes in and lives in our heart, but the soulish part of us, which is our mind, will, and emotions need to be renewed by the word of God.

Romans 12:2 says *And be not conformed to this world but be ye transformed by the renewing of your mind, that ye may prove what is that good, and acceptable, and perfect, will of God.* The word *conformed* in Greek means to conform to same pattern, to same fashion. In Webster dictionary, it means the form of a person or thing is its shape. To conform is to fit in with others in form, shape, or manner. In other words, God is telling us not to be conformed, fashioned, or shaped according to the evil of this world in its thinking and doings, but allow the transforming of our mind (its mental faculties, reason, or understanding) according to word of God and when we do this, then we will know the good, acceptable, and perfect will of God. While attending church service, the Lord spoke to me about this baby I was carrying. He told me if I would have it, that she would be the greatest blessing to me. When Pastor said that, I didn't believe; he really knew what he was saying. In fact, it was an answer to a prayer. When I found out that I was pregnant and possibly having my stepfather's baby, I remember telling God *how could I raise this child up and give it the love it needed, when my own life was in such turmoil? What if it was my stepdad and it came out looking like him, will she be a daily reminder of the sexual abuse I had to experience at the hands of my father?* All these thoughts would bombard my mind. The more I felt this living being growing in me, the more I fell in love with her. Besides, this would be the one person that will love me no matter what. All she would see is her mother. Holy Spirit continued to speak to me about coming clean with my past. Just picturing the thought of coming clean, fear started to grip me. If you got pregnant through incest, rape or violation and you aborted the child because you just could not bear giving birth to the child because he/she would be a constant reminder of your abuser, there are consequences. Let's look at the spiritual repercussions of having an abortion, either willingly or unwillingly. According to Bible.org, some of us are encouraged to have an abortion because family members encouraged it due to selfishness, shame, and fear that it would bring on family. You may have physically aborted a baby but the emotional torment will not be so easy to forget. Most women that didn't want to have an abortion felt the pressure of circumstance causes them to do so.

The Bible says we were all born in sin and shapen in iniquity (Psalm 51:5). Because the child was born via sexual abuse, you must understand that that child came to earth just when God needed it to be here, regardless of what situation you might have been. God has a plan and purpose for that child and for you. Satan hates anything that is created in God's own image. Most post-abortive women are plagued by guilt, and have outburst of rage, while some go into a state of denial, trying to suppress the problem, but it eventually pops back up. While millions of women go into depression and are suicidal, they hide behind alcohol, drugs, or promiscuity to try not to remember the horrific ordeal. Going down the baby aisle, or passing a newborn baby in shopping cart, anything that pertains to a baby makes them cry and it is a constant trigger of their abortion. It is crucial that you know that abortion is not the unpardonable sin. Jesus Christ died to pay all our sins and wrong decisions we have made, including abortion. He extends cleansing and forgiveness to every woman who has been wounded by an abortion.   Jesus offers reconciliation with God and the grace to forgive. No sin is so great that the blood or love of Christ can't forgive. There is peace, forgiveness, and cleansing from guilt in the blood of Jesus. I had to clear my conscience and tell my fiancé at time the truth. How would I handle the rejection? I had enough of that in my life. So, here I go. I got the courage to tell him, and it didn't go quite like I wanted it. I was expecting a fight, an argument, pans flying across my head but that didn't happen. Yes, he was disappointed but he said, "I forgive you." Our relationship ended that day. But I still had my mother and my stepfather to approach. I had approached my mother. I tried so many times to tell her before but she just didn't have the time, but this time, she was going to listen. I got the nerve to tell her the whole story. We had a mother-daughter talk that day for the first time ever, and she listened to me. She apologizes for not being there and was very sorry.

3rd, I had to find my abuser. Most people wouldn't even want anything to do with their abuser but I had questions that needed answers. So, I found him. I made sure I stood close by the door in case I had to run. I looked him in the eyes and I asked him one question, "Why?" Why did you do all those horrible things to me? You messed my life up. He turned his face to a wall because he couldn't even look at me; he turned back around with regret in his eyes and said, "I'm sorry." A weight lifted off my shoulder. For just a moment, I felt free. I asked him if he was ever abused as a child; he said, "Yes." You see, hurting people hurt other people. For just one moment, we had something in common. I forgave him that day. I prayed the sinner's prayer with him that day and that God would heal hearts. I couldn't persecute him because the Statue of Limitation had ended. When I last heard, he was suffering from health issues. Growing up, I would never have allowed my daughter to go around my stepfather, her father, because of the fear of him hurting her.

When my daughter got to a certain age where she started asking questions, I told her the truth and why I never wanted her to go out alone with her father. I would allow her to talk to him on the phone and he would pay child support. It was just like God told me; she has been the greatest blessing to me. She has stuck by me, helped me in my business, and supported me. She has truly blessed my life.

There is a story in 2 Samuel 13:1-22. Amnon was a half-brother of Tamar. Amnon becomes King David first biological son after David's first son by Bathsheba dies. Maacah is the third wife of King David, and they bore two children—Tamar and Absalom. Maacah was a daughter of King Talmai of the kingdom of Geshur. That makes Tamar a princess of a royal descendant. According to one translation, Tamar being of royal descendant and a virgin, was closely watched by harem eunuchs. She lived in a woman's quarter and couldn't go outside the walls unless accompanied by other woman or a guard. Tamar was a beautiful woman to look at, that one translation says Amnon would watch Tamar as she went about her everyday duties as a princess. This is why in verse two, it said it was hard for Amnon to get hold of Tamar because she was well-guarded. The devil had put into Amnon's heart to lust after his own sister.

In Leviticus 18:1-18, God talks to his people about sexual purity and how we are not to sleep with close relatives. The door to sexual perversion had opened in David's family when he lusted after Bathsheba as she was bathing and decided to have her for himself. David had Bathsheba's husband killed in battle and made sure he was positioned in battle where he knew he would be killed. Because of this sin, David and Bathsheba's first child together would die. Amnon's lust for his own sister is unnatural that he became sick over her because he couldn't get close to her. In verse 2, it says he was vexed over her. The word *vexed* in Dictionary.com translation means to torment, trouble, distress, plaque, worry, irritate, annoy, or provoke. Amnon had a friend named Jonadab who was very crafty man. The word *crafty* in Webster's dictionary means deceitful or sly. In another translation, it means clever at achieving one's aim by direct or deceitful methods. In Merriam Webster's dictionary, it means attaining or seeking to attain one's end by guileful or devious means.

Genesis 3:1 says the serpent was crafty than any other wild animals. Jonadab who exemplified the same behavior as the serpent, had come up with a plan to get Tamar in the same room as Amnon. Jonadab brought to Amnon's attention that Amnon is still a prince and son of a King. He should, therefore, use his position as the King's first son to get what he desires. When King David came, and found Amnon sick, Amnon suggested Tamar should come and cook for him but all that was a plot to get her to himself. Following protocol, Tamar did obey what the King asked of her. She went in a virgin and came out an abused woman. Alone, unguarded, and no way to fend for herself, he forces himself on her. When he grabbed hold of her, I could imagine the surprise and fear on Tamar's face when she finally realizes the real reason Amnon ask for her. With her heart pounding and in total disbelief of what was happening, Tamar pleaded with him to think about the consequences that this action would bring on her and him as she fought and wrestled with him. But Amnon ignored all her pleadings. She even suggested to him to go to King David and ask for her hand in marriage knowing that David would not consent to such a thing because according to Levitical law, it was unlawful for relatives to marry each other. This was Tamar's attempt to dissuade Amnon and it would give him time to come to his sense. There was no reasoning with Amnon as he carried out this horrific and selfish act.

After the act was done, Amnon hated her. The difference between lust and love is this: Lust when it is fulfilled brings forth a shame and guilt, but love is patient, love is kind, it doesn't envy, it doesn't boast, it is not proud, it doesn't dishonor others, it's not self-seeking, it's not easily angered, it keeps no record of wrong, love doesn't delight in evil but rejoice with the truth, always protects, always trust, always hopes, always perseveres. Love never fails. (1 Corinthians 13:4-8; NIV). When someone forces themselves on you and make you do things you don't want to do, that is lust. Lust is all about who I can have power over and who I can control.

Notice that after Amnon was done taking her virginity, he hated and kicked her out. When a person hates themselves because of an act or deed done wrong to an individual, such an act is normally expressed on the victim of the deed or act. He hated her because he hated himself due to what he did to her. Now, guilt and shame has kicked in. In verse 16, Tamar is still pleading with Ammon. He never even acknowledge what he did to her. No apology, pleas, or request for forgiveness. He took no responsibility for his action at all; it went in one ear and out the other. When David found out, the Bible said he was angry, yet, David never confronts Amnon on what he did. David who dropped Goliath to his knees with a rock and slingshot, slew tens of thousands, and took the foreskin of 200 Philistines, did nothing to protect Tamar. The very people that was supposed to be there for you, protect you, and support you, should be your parents, but David did nothing about it. He didn't even investigate the situation to even see what had happen. On top of that, Tamar's brother, Absalom, told her to be quiet about the matter. After all, it was her brother. We don't want it to get out; we got to protect the family's name.

The devil used secrecy as a means of remaining hidden to isolate its victims to destroy them. Family secrets can destroy the person holding the secret until you start to tell on it. It will keep you bound. When we read further down, Absalom probably wanted Tamar not to say anything because he was contemplating a plan to have Amnon killed and that would make him heir to the throne. Everybody was worried about themselves, protecting themselves and what they could get out of the situation, except being concerned about Tamar and how she must be feeling. She needed their love and support. What a burden Tamar had to carry. As she rent her garments of many colors, which represents favor and royalty, and pour ashes on her head which represents grief and humiliation, her face in her hands represent the shame she would have to suffer for the rest of her life. You never heard from Tamar again after this act. She went into desolation in her brother Absalom's home. How many of you reading this are Tamar? You never told anyone about your sexual abuse. You try to cover it up with alcohol, drugs, men, sex, money, and things of this world but can never hide your pain. It will always pop back up if you don't deal with it. It's kinda like if you take a ball and push it down in water, what happens? It pops right back up until you deal with it. These things are temporary solutions. Why not give it to God and let Him heal and mend your life. Get off the treadmill of Insanity. Insanity is doing the same thing over and over and expecting different results. Get your power back; take your life back. Life is too short; you only have one life to live, so live it to the fullest.

In the Old Testament and culture of that time, monetary compensation was given in order for that victim to gain some dignity. Rape and incest is something that is not new to our society. It's been going on for centuries. Let's look at other stories in the Bible where rape occurred. In Genesis 19:30-35, Lot's daughters got him drunk and took turns raping him to produce a male seed. Shechem raped Dinah by force in Genesis 34:1-2. The men of Gibeah ganged raped a Levite concubine, brutalized her until she literally died in Judges 19:25.

Many victims of rape and incest go into denial to keep themselves from remembering what happened to them. This is called repressed memory. Wikipedia describes it as memories that have been unconsciously blocked due to the memory being associated with a high level of stress or trauma. It is sometimes compared to the term dissociative amnesia, which is defined in the DSM-V as an inability to recall autobiographical information. Luke 12:2 says there is nothing that is hidden that will not be exposed. So, it's better to deal with your trauma or it will show through memory loss and affect your emotions or manifest itself in your body through sickness or disease. If you don't deal with the memory of sexual abuse, the enemy will use it to torment you by entering your mind and causing traumatic shock emotionally as a result of being violated by a person you trusted.

Many people in our society today that never dealt with this trauma find themselves in psychiatric wards, killed themselves, have outbursts of anger, and find themselves in jail or imprisoned because of murder. It reminded them of their abuser, or they even killed their abuser. If you are in jail because you killed or assaulted your abuser, it's never okay to assault another person or take another person's life. Forgive yourself, and forgive your abuser. It wasn't easy at first for me to forgive my abuser. For myself, I had to forgive by faith because God said so. Carrying hate in my heart, I was only hurting myself. Remember what I said in the previous verses that there is no greater avenger than God Himself. When it looks like that person is getting a get-out-of-jail-free card, there is going to come a day when something will happen to that person if they don't repent and ask for forgiveness. We are all going to stand before the judgment seat of Christ.

The Bible says we should bless those that curse us and pray for those that despitefully use us (Luke 6:28). The thing is, for you to walk in the freedom that you have in Christ and choose not to be a victim anymore. Release the person over to God. If you still hold on to your abuser, Satan can keep you bound up to your past and debar you from walking into your future with victory. Jeremiah 29:11, *For I know the plans I have for you says the Lord, plans to prosper you and not to harm you, plans to give you hope and a future.* Isn't it wonderful to know that even when enemies try their best to take us out, God's plans for our life is secure? Hallelujah!!!

Chapter 7

Signs and Statistics

Apostle Ivory Hopkins' book, *Deliverance From Spirits of Sexual Abuse*, says that sexual predators normally go after victims who are insecure, shy, quiet, rejected, suicidal, or have been sexually abused. These types of victims are easily manipulated and controlled by their victimizer. Sexual predators are sex addicts and need deliverance because they use sex to feed the hurt, wounds, and emptiness inside of them. Sexual predators must now register as a sex offender called Megan's Law. You can go online and see if there are sexual offenders in your area.

According to RAINN (Rape, Abuse & Incest National Network), statistics show that 44% of Victims of Sexual Abuse are under the age of 18. Every 98 seconds, a person is sexually assaulted. 68% of sexual abuser never report their abuser; therefore, the abuser go scot-free, and sexual assault is the most underreported crime. Approximately four out of five assaults are committed by someone known by the victim—a father, brother, friend, babysitter, pastor or by someone that is an acquaintance. 98% of sexual predators will never spend a day in jail or prison because of shame and facing their accuser in court is like repeating the trauma again for the victim. The effects of sexual assaults undergo depression, post-traumatic stress, alcohol abuse, drug abuse, and suicide contemplation. In 2012, over 17,000 pregnancies were as a result of rape. I write these statistics so that the victims can see that they are not the only one affected by this kind of violence. I am sharing my testimony along with others of sexual abuse to get the message out to the victim so that they are not alone and they too can overcome it.

Because sexual abuse started with me at a young age by several members in my family, I want to list some warning signs just in case you run into someone that may be expressing the warnings signs listed below. As I have said previously, these signs are not always systems of abuse and could be something else causing these systems.

- Nightmares
- Sudden mood changes: fear, rage, insecurity or withdrawal
- Develop new or unusual fear of people or places
- Become clingy: don't want you to leave them alone
- Draw pictures, writes, or dreams of sexual or frightening images
- Fear of talking about a secret he/she shares with an adult or another person
- Become quiet or secluded suddenly
- Fear of the dark
- Bedwetting or thumb-sucking
- Exhibits adult sexual behavior
- Resist removing clothes at bath time, diaper change, toileting
- Running away from home

These are by no means to an end, and these signs are not limited to sexual abuse but could be something else. A lot of these signs mentioned are what happened to me in my childhood days.

Physical Signs

- Pain, discoloration, bleeding or discharge in genitals
- Persistent or recurring pain and burning during urination
- Swelling and redness in the genital area
- Walking as if he/she is having pain or discomfort

Chapter 8

Conclusion

Before I conclude this book, let me kill the myth that when someone is sexually abused, they too tend to become an abuser. This is not always the case. I would never think of touching my children, grandchildren and any other person's child I am in contact with in any manner that is inappropriate. Some people do go on to abuse others. This is called the spirit of a sexual predator. This type of spirit operates in a sexual abuser, who victimizes another for his or her sexual, demonic pleasure. Along with this spirit are spirits of lust, emotional damage (they were abused themselves), spirits of pain, pornography, rape spirits, and child molesting spirits, hatred of women or men, spirit of fantasy, with bound and blocked conscience, according to Ivory Hopkins' book on deliverance from the spirits of sexual abuse (pg. 25). Apostle Hopkins is one of my mentor I've been following for over a year now, and he has written some phenomenal books about this issue. I might not be under his ministry, but every time I read one of his manuals on any subject, he is mentoring me.

I hope that those buying this book will find encouragement and hope to come out of despair and isolation and find the light that Christ offers. He is the only one that can bring salvation, healing, and deliverance for you. I am a testimony to you today that you can find victory and freedom that you need. It took messages like this to come out of my despair and find the voice that the enemy wanted to silence. For some of you reading this book, it may not be as easy as this. You may need to visit a Christian counselor who can counsel you with the natural and spiritual side of things because what you've been through includes a lot more than sexual abuse, but you have been through trauma in your life that can cause mental illness because you have repressed the memory of your abuse causing bound or blocked memory. Trauma is any shock, wound, or bodily injury that can either be remembered or repressed, depending on needs, your age, and nature of the trauma.

Apostle Ivory Hopkins, in his book, *Deliverance From Spirits of Sexual Abuse.*, page 4&5, says many victims often go into denial or block the rape out of their memory. Forgetting is one of the ways many victims try to overcome the bondage of sexual abuse, but the body or emotions will bring it up. The body bring it up via pain and infirmities, while the emotions by psychological problems or addictions. Luke 12:2: *For there is nothing covered, that shall not be revealed, neither hid, that shall not be known*. The rape, abuse or molestation can cause the memory to lose thoughts. Repressed memory is a way the mind protects itself for a while because it was never meant for the mind to shut down in this, leaving you free to focus your conscious energy on here and now. Get the help that you need. It is okay to bring in a third person that can help and walk you through the process of trauma. Find churches that offer deliverance in your region, who can cast out demonic spirits out of you and loose you from any soul ties to your abuser and people you have had sex with that can keep you bound up. I also went through some self-deliverance. Apostle John Eckhart has a book called *Prayers that Rout Demons*, that you can speak over yourself and cast out demonic spirits. Some churches don't offer this type of ministry to its people. You may have to do what I did. I had to travel to conferences outside of my region because my region didn't offer it. If you're desperate enough to want to be free, you will seek it out for yourself. Today, I can say that God isn't finished with me yet. I have come a long way and I'm not where I used to be. I know who I am and Who I believe in. My identity is in who I am in Christ. I am going to shout it to the world, and not be silent anymore. I tell the devil to get out of my way because everything he stole from me in previous season when I didn't know who I was, I'm coming to get them. If he gets in my way, well I'm just going to have to run him over!!! Isaiah 60:1 is what I will end on. *Arise and Shine, for your light has come and the glory of the Lord has risen upon you*. It's time, ladies, to step into the light. This is your time to be a victim no more. The Lord has a place and platform for you; put your coat back on, the coat that represents glory, beauty, and royalty. You are fearfully and wonderfully made by God. You are a child of the King. You are a Queen; you just lost your identity for just a minute. But I say, Rise!!! Daughter of the King, Rise and take your place; a place no one can walk in except you.

Rise!!! The world is waiting for your voice, the world is waiting for your debut, and the time is NOW!!!!!!

www.ingramcontent.com/pod-product-compliance
Lightning Source LLC
Chambersburg PA
CBHW031422250726
48656CB00002B/779